MW00523125

Manipulation And Dark Psychology

Everything You Need To Know About How To Influence People With Persuasion, Nlp, Dark Psychology And Mind Control

Written By

Richard Neel

Table of Contents

INTRODUCTION

Thank you for purchasing this book!

Dark Psychology plays major roles in the world of Criminology. When you are trying to catch a criminal, it is easier if you understand how they think. Therefore, it is easy
to see why these three things go hand in hand. Getting into the mind of a criminal, killer, or rapist can be very difficult for those of us that do not have these extremely dark tendencies. So, the fact that there is information accumulating for us to research is critical.

It is hard to wrap your brain around how a human being can be wired so much differently. Until we find the ability to do this, it can make catching the really bad guys difficult. With advances in understanding the darker tendencies of human nature it has become easier for Criminologists, Police Officers, and others to find these ugly individuals.

Psychology, and in turn, Dark Psychology have been around for a very long time. In fact, as far back as histories go, there have been people working on understanding why humans do what they do. We all have the capability of doing bad things. Some of us have a much easier time doing these non-moral acts above others.

Finding examples of people from the past to the present day that have the qualities studied in Dark Psychology is easy. It doesn't matter what time frame you look at, you will be able to pick out the characteristics easily with a few, obvious examples. Once you see it on a large scale you can start to look at the people around you every day and see some of the same features. It is actually quite unsettling to realize how many people around you are prone to dark desires.

One of the most obvious examples is Adolf Hitler. Obviously, he committed awful acts. However, he had more than an entire country under his thumb. Why is that? Well, he was charismatic, he spoke

articulately, and he was an amazing manipulator. He completely understood what he needed to do to have control over the masses.

He built a core group of like-minded people to help him along the way. While these people had a better look at what the truth was behind his tactics, we can't believe they knew everything. A person such as Adolf Hitler would never let all of their secrets out. When looking for a prime example of a person that falls into all three categories of the Dark Triad, he is perfect.

With fear, power, charisma, likability, and laser focus he managed to convince his people to commit atrocious acts against humanity. It's odd to think that on an individual level, his followers were normal good people. When bombarded with propaganda, well-thought out words, and intimidation they bent to the will of a madman.

If people were better able to understand what was driving Hitler, there could have been a stop to his reign much more quickly.

Enjoy your reading!

What Is Manipulation

Manipulation is where the individual will work to get what they want, often using covert and underhand tricks. They see the other person in the relationship (whether it is a

romantic relationship, familiar relationship, friendship, or someone at work) simply as a tool that they can use to get their way. They often don't care if they end up harming the other person in the process or not, as long as they get what they want.

Different types of manipulation are sometimes used to an agreement or help someone mutually beneficial to both parties. But when it comes to dark psychology, manipulation helps just the manipulator and no one else in the process. Many techniques can be used with manipulation—including foot in the door, intimidation, lying, love bombing, and more.

In dark psychology, the dark triad is often going to talk about psychopathy, Machiavellianism, and narcissism. These will be known as dark traits because of some of the evil parts that go with them. Research on these traits is used in a field known as applied psychology—especially when we are looking into business management, clinical psychology, and law enforcement. People who test for and then end up scoring high on these kinds of traits are the most likely to commit crimes, cause trouble in society, and create problems inside a business if hired, especially when they land a leadership role.

All three of these dark traits will be conceptually distinct from one another, although evidence shows that they easily will overlap sometimes.

They are going to be associated with a personality type that is very manipulative and callous towards others, which can make it hard for them to have close friends or anyone at all who wants to do something with them at any time.

To help us understand these a bit more and see what the personality traits are all about and why we want to mention them in dark psychology.

Machiavellianism

The first trait of the dark triad that we will take a look at is known as Machiavellianism. The trait was first given name after the political philosophy promoted by Niccolò Machiavelli. If someone scores high with this kind of trait, they will be very cynical, which means that they will be skeptical of others and be more interested in the self than others, even in an unethical way.

Also, scoring high with this kind of personality trait will mean that the person is dishonest and cold. They believe that the way to success is interpersonal manipulation with pretty much everyone they meet, and because of these thoughts, they are going to act accordingly.

This kind of person has an idea of what they want in life, and they don't care what it is going to take to get that thing. If they have to walk all over people, manipulate others, and cause trouble, they will do it. Keeping up with what they will do next to get what they want is going to be hard.

Narcissism

The next thing that we need to take a look at is the idea of narcissism. Individuals who end up scoring high with this particular trait will display a lot of superiority, dominance, entitlement, and grandiosity in everything they do.

With this one, you will run across someone who doesn't even comprehend that other people have feelings and thoughts, and they act in the manner they do because of this misunderstanding.

To the narcissist, other people are simply tools that they can use for their benefit. They don't care whether the other person is hurt on the way to success, and often they assume that others think and react to the world in the same way that they do. They will often hold onto their target for a long time because it allows them to do what they want without searching for another person to give them constant praise and attention. But since they have no care for how the other person is treated, this target, especially if they stay in the relationship for a long period, will end up with mental and emotional problems.

Psychopathy

Compared to the other two parts of this triad, psychopathy will be seen as the three's evilest. Individuals who score high on this kind of issue will show very low empathy levels and higher thrill-seeking and impulsivity levels. This means that when a psychopath wants something, they want to do it right now, and they don't have much care for the thoughts or feelings of the other people around them at all. Often, this will be even lower than what we would see with the other two options.

Researchers have found a similarity that shows up between those who have antisocial personality disorder and psychopathy, so this will need to be explored more in the future. This is seen as one of the worst conditions out of the three, and without proper care, it can cause a lot of issues along the way with interpersonal relationships.

The dark triad can cause many workplace problems, in society, and in any relationship that becomes a part of it. They may be in love with the dark psychologist and want to see what it takes to make things work, but often, the dark psychologist has no want or need to make things right.

As long as the target continues doing what they should, even when the target gets hurt, the dark psychologist will keep on with the same course of action, getting what they want in the process.

Mind Control

It is a system of influences that come into play to disrupt the individual on a significant level. The hope is to shake up the individual so much that you can get to their core and change up their identity, putting in a brand-new identity in its place, one that the manipulator will design to fit their needs. It can sometimes be used in beneficial ways. Some mind control techniques help change the addict's personality and help them get over their addiction. But here, we will take a look more at the uses of mind control that force the individual to change to benefit the manipulator, not anything that will benefit the target. According to a psychologist known as Philip Zimbardo, mind control will be the process where the individual action and choice will be compromised by agents or agencies trying to modify things like cognition, affect, motivation, perception, and behavioral outcomes. And it is believed that everyone, no matter who they are and their background could be susceptible at some point to this manipulation.

With mind control, it will not be some ancient mystery that only a few people know about. It will be a combination of words and even group pressures that makes the manipulator create dependency on those who use it. The manipulator will gain full control and make decisions for those they control, while the target assumes that they still have the freedom to decide. This is part of mind control; the target is not aware of the influence process or even its changes.

There are techniques you can use to execute some influence over other people around you. And often, when you are using these with the ideas of dark psychology, you are planning on using them to gain your benefit without worrying about how it can influence or harm another person.

Persuasion

Persuasion is something that we experience daily. We are going to be persuaded by friends and family to help out on occasion. We will see many advertisements from companies that want to persuade us to purchase their products and not from competitors. We see persuasion so often that it is sometimes hard to realize that it could be bad and that a manipulator could try to use this against us.

When it comes to persuasion, Robert Cialdini is well respected for some of his ideas on persuasion and how to do it successfully, whether your intentions are good or not.

According to Cialdini, six principles can be used to help out with the ideas of persuasion, and these six principles are going to include:

Reciprocity: This is where you will do a small favor for someone, and then right away, ask them to do one back.

Commitment and consistency: It holds the target of doing something because they have done it in the past.

Social proof: This is when you convince the target to do something because it is popular, and everyone is doing it.

Authority: Your target is more likely to do something if they believe you are an authority on that topic.

Likeability: If you can become likable and see you as a friend, they are more likely to do what you ask.

Scarcity: This is the fear that an item will be in short supply, so they want to get it.

There are persuasive techniques to get hold of your target and get them to do what you want while they still believe they have full control over their thoughts and actions at this time.

Deception

Another technique that a dark psychologist can use is known as deception. This will refer back to the act, whether it is kind or cruel or big or small, of causing another person, your target, to believe something that is not true. Even those who are pretty honest will practice this deception at some time, and it is believed that the average person will lie at least a few times a day, even if the lies are not big and won't harm the other person.

There are many ways to lie about things to the other person, but it is usually to hide some information from the target to react in the manner that the manipulator wants. This makes sure that the target will react the way the manipulator wants without really knowing why it would be the wrong decision. The manipulator gets what they want because they told an outright lie or hid some information, and often the target will be hurt in the process because of this.

Differences between Persuasion and Manipulation?

Truly, these two concepts are very closely related and most people get confused between their differences and meanings and the line between them seems blurred. It is crucial for you

to figure out when you are crossing the line of persuasion and entering into the manipulation zone. Hence, before understanding what is the difference between them, let us first understand the meaning of them which would clear out the difference automatically.

Persuasion means when you say or act in such a way that people do or believe what you are saying. Persuasion is something that we do every day on a daily basis. Persuasion is never taken in an evil or negative way. We can say that it is the way we interact with the people who are around us. At times while discussing any topic when we try to keep our point and prove ourselves right, that as well is persuasion. It also comes into the picture when you want someone to do something right and want to see this world as a better place. Also, at times you try to persuade people when you want to earn a profit or sell a product and doing this is not being wicked or doing something immoral.

Let us understand this by taking an example when you make a product according to the customer's needs and requirements and want to make the journey of the buyer easy and then you are trying to convince them to buy it as you know it will benefit them and you both.

Now, let us understand what manipulation means. It means the act to change by unfair or artful means to serve your purpose. In manipulation, you are not bothered about the other person's benefit or less what you want to see is your revenue and benefit. In this case, you

want your profit no matter what, by any means. If in case the buyer as well is benefiting then that is good but they are not concerned about that. Manipulation always comprises of deception and misrepresentation of the product or truth, but it does not go a long way.

Most of the researchers say that the difference between the two comes down to basically three things which are-

a) The intention behind your persuasion

b) Transparency and truthfulness behind your desire

c) A benefit to the other person

- These were the major differences between persuasion and manipulation. Yes, there is a very thin line of intention between them, but it is important for you to realize it. Persuasion is always positive and manipulations are said to be negative and evil. With the help of persuasion in an argument, you try to make the interlocutor adopt your point of view, on the other hand, in manipulation; you bent the truth to get approval from the interlocutor. In persuasion, the opponent willingly accepts your point but in manipulation, the person is coerced to agree.

- Persuasion is usually done with the intention to do good things. Here you would try to recommend the buyer with the best services and try to make the perfect match and also would strive that the person stops using anything which is harmful. On the contrary in manipulation, only one of the parties is benefited

- In persuasion, you present all the right arguments in the best manner which are logical and convincing both but in manipulation people try to mold the truth so that they can achieve their selfish goals

- Although, in persuasion as well you try to convince others when they do not agree with your point. But the thing is that you are being transparent and the intentions are good and real. On the other hand, manipulation is opposite

- In persuasion, if the other person agrees to what you were trying to tell they would benefit from it as it was in their favor. But in manipulation, the other person would regret after agreeing to your point. The reason behind it is that the truth was not told; the customer had no benefit as the intent was never good.

I am sure by now it must be very clear to you that what does both these things mean and what are the major differences in them. Therefore, you should always think while convincing someone that does it benefit just you or the other person as well. It will become easy for you to understand whether you are doing something wrong or you are right.

Don't you think persuasion is a really good technique and every one of us should imply it in our lives and think about ours and others benefits too? So, let us learn a few persuasion tactics which would help you in changing other's mind-

- Scarcity Technique- This is the most used persuasion technique and mostly the salesman and marketers use it. I am sure that you must have seen that the product which is less in supply, people tend to ask more of it. Thus, if you want to increase the demand for your product or service always show that it is available for a limited time or the offer is just for the time being, it would increase the chances of an increase in sales of your product. You must have read these lines many times such as never to be seen again, once a year, attaching a timer, limited offer, etc. Also, there was an experiment done where one group was given a product which was in great amount and the other group was given a product which was scarce. The end of this experiment was the second group could sell more products as people were keen to buy it because it was limited. You as well can use this tactic to increase the demand for your commodities.

- Social Authentication- People usually consider this technique as it does not take time to notice that in social groups people usually there are group thinkers of higher level. Whenever anyone thinks of a unique idea whatever everyone agrees or not but yes they think and give their point of view. So, whenever you take any decision, in that regard you will always consider the points that your mates or friends mentioned. For example, there are many people who just start smoking either because for them it is social proof or their friends too so they also start doing it.

- Reciprocation- Most of the people like returning favors if someone does something good for them. Also, majorly people do not even know that they would like the gift or not they are just inclined to return the favor back. If you make someone feel indebted that is a good way increases the probability of getting what you desire. For example, you want to collect money for some old age people so that they can get a house. Instead of directly asking for money, according to their talent, you can ask them to make beautiful frames, pots, etc. Give them to people, make them feel indebted and then ask for a donation. Also, a study was done and seen the more kind the waiter was to the customers the more tip he got. So, be generous to all and they would in turn return generosity towards you.

- Authority- If you want to convince people always to show yourself as a source of authority. Most people look up to authority or a leader be it any field and get easily

  convinced when an authoritative person says something. For example, if you read that 9 out of 10 doctors recommend using a specific brand of soap, then most of the people would run after that brand as it has gained an advantage over others. This states that the majority of the people follow someone who has authority, at times even when they are wrong. This technique explains to you that always be confident and have your own attitude if you want people to follow you or get influenced by what you say or do.

- Regularity and commitment- It has been seen that people who show regularity and fulfill the promises then it helps them in influencing others to do more for them. Such as if you fulfill the commitment and do what you said in time, it influences others and makes them believe that they can count on you and can help you in persuasion when you want them to do something for you. For example, many websites instead of writing signup, use the statement like- join me and the second option is No, I am boring. Statements like this convince customers and it increases their conversion rates.

- Foot in the door- This persuasion technique is very interesting and many people use it. This technique states that whenever you want a favor from someone, first ask for a smaller one and then ask for the bigger favor. It means that when you first ask for help and if the person says yes, they get committed to doing that and when you ask for the bigger help it can act as a continuation for the smaller one. For example, if you fail a test and your teacher says no to taking the test again. You should first always ask for feedback so that you can work on it. And then request the teacher whether they can take the test again. This way the teacher would see that you are really keen to learn and improve and would not say no.

- Door in the Face- Well, this technique has been seen in many stores and supermarkets. It is the opposite of the technique mentioned above. In this method, you first ask for big favors and if the person says no then request and ask if they can do something easy and small for you. This way the other person gets convinced and thinks that if not a big help but yes then can do a favor by doing something small. For example, you ask your cousin or any mate for Rs.10, 000 if they say no then you can always say that if not 10,000 can you please help me with Rs. 3000. There are major possibilities that they would say yes.
- Anchoring- This is said to one of the most powerful persuasion methods. It has numerous uses but is mostly used in pricing. This technique can be best explained with the help of an example. You go to the market to buy a refrigerator for yourself, the salesman says Rs. 30,999 but you bargain and get the cost lowered to Rs.27, 500. You would be happy that you got a great deal and feel satisfied, instead of knowing that the actual price of it was maybe less than that. But you

are happy as according to you it was the best deal.

Mental Control

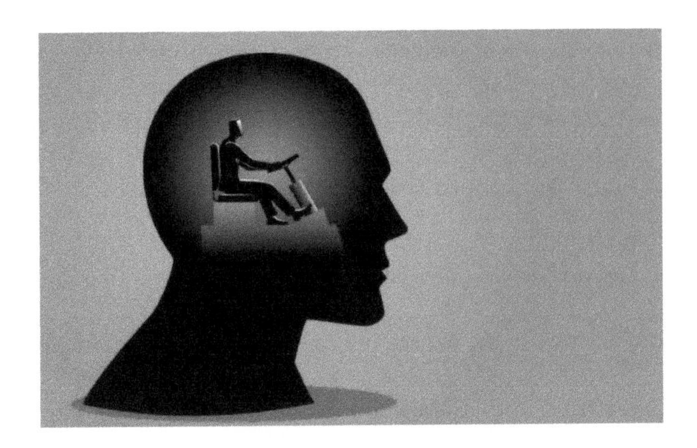

Another concentration in the field of dark psychology research is mental control. It can be a piece of both control and influence as the two strategies reach within your psyche and

attempt to get you to accomplish something, think something, or tail another person's way for you. For some individuals, mental control can mean various things, such as control, influence, impact, and indoctrination. We will see mental control as an approach to change an individual's contemplations, convictions and control their activities.

Numerous individuals accept that brain control is one of the most all- around shrouded types of impact because the vast majority is not even mindful; it is occurring. It is additionally a reasonable procedure, which makes it harder for individuals to take note. Individuals under psyche control will feel that they are settling on their choice, yet another person makes these choices. You should know that the time allotment it takes to control somebody's brain relies upon the used strategies: their character, individual elements, and social elements. Now and then, mental control can happen in light of physical power.

Like control and influence, mental control used in our regular day to day existence. For the most part, we are unconscious that the strategies publicizing organizations use are a type of brain control. In any case, when they can get us to accept that their item is the best; this is what they are doing. It doesn't imply that you have to know what the promotion organizations are doing consistently. The mental control you should know about is the dark kind. You should know about mental control when it can negatively hurt you. Focusing on

promotions is an excellent method to rehearse how to monitor you against mental control and get what procedures are being used.

Ways You Can Control People or Be Controlled

Individuals who need to control their brain can utilize any of the accompanying methods or systems that fall under control or influence. One of the most significant variables to recollect is individuals who control others are incredible at understanding individuals. They can ordinarily determine what sort of individual they are managing before long. It encourages them to recognize what kind of system they can utilize and which one they can't. It also enables them to comprehend what kind of individual you are. They have to know whether you have a ton of enthusiastic and mental quality, as this can make their activity harder. They need to see if you have high confidence or affected.

Conduct Molding and Conditioning

Conduct molding, otherwise called alteration, is the way to get individuals to do what you need. You do this through a progression of remunerations and disciplines. It is used in child-rearing classes and brain research courses in school. You have to understand that behavior adjustment is the demonstration of changing somebody's conduct. When the individual reliably follows the behavior they were instructed, it is known as social molding. A social alteration will consistently precede conduct molding.

Individuals who need to assume responsibility for your mind exceed expectations at behavior change. This is because they have to change your conduct to condition you, which is the point at which they have entirely control. They have to ensure that opposition towards the changing practices is negligible. They will wind up battling with molding. You may likewise get on to their brain control inclinations and do what you can to end it.

Conviction Change Processes

Perhaps the greatest key to altering somebody's perspective is you have to concentrate on changing their conviction forms. This implies you not just change their conviction; you change the thinking behind it.

Probably the greatest subject that mental controllers are acceptable at is brain research. A brain controller will consider how their objective thinks to deal with their points of view. This causes them to open an entryway into controlling their objective's brain. This makes specialists probably the best model with regard to mental control. In any case, advisors are attempting to enable their customers to change practices to better their lives. Mental controllers need to change their objective's rules so that they can acquire control over the individual.

Undercover Belief Changes

You don't have to utilize pictures to get somebody to change their convictions. Most brain controllers, who are attempting to control you to pick up the high ground, won't center on pictures. This is because you will get on too effectively, particularly from the outset. This doesn't mean they will never place-specific images in your mind. It just implies that they will, in general, spotlight more on clandestine conviction changes.

Psyche controllers should ensure that they have your trust, regard, and an association with them. Without these variables, they won't have the option to significant change your convictions. They are additionally talented at tying down. This is because they understand that feelings are regularly a reliable guide for individuals and don't know how to control their emotions. For individuals who can keep up their feelings well, mental controllers will battle to get effective through this technique.

The initial step for the psyche controller will lead you to the conduct they need to change. At the point when they do this, they will attempt to be inconspicuous in their endeavors. They won't act like they need

to change your conduct straightforwardly. Nonetheless, they could refer to how it affected them as this will evoke an enthusiastic reaction from you.

When you give them a feeling, they will pull out the mooring method. Whatever conduct they need you to transform, they will quietly provide you what you ought to do. While this probably won't work quickly, you will begin to change your conduct. You will remember how you felt when you talked each time you do what your life partner feels isn't right. After some time, you will quit partaking in this conduct increasingly since it gives you a negative inclination.

Rewards and Consequences

It is now challenging for grown-ups to get a handle because they get prizes and consequences for their activities. This happens a few times each day, yet we once in a while pay attention to it. For instance, if you complete an undertaking, your manager will compliment you. If you can't finish the assignment by the cutoff time and need to request an expansion, you will hear the failure in their voice. This will make a negative outcome, which will make you increasingly mindful of time on the board. You will be bound to make cutoff times later on.

Mental controllers will likewise follow the prizes and result framework. If you go out with your companions when your loved one disclosed to you, they didn't generally require you to, they will give you the silent treatment for two or three days. This will cause you to understand that they are baffled by you, which will make you disillusioned in yourself. While you probably won't comprehend why they are doing this as you just went out with a few companions, your feelings will manage you more than your considerations. When your better half discloses to you, they would prefer you to remain at home than go out; you are bound to consider staying at home. This doesn't mean you will.

The I to You Shift

This is basic in the usual discussion, which implies it very well, maybe not easy to spot. Nonetheless, individuals who are attempting to control their brain will regularly move their story onto you. This implies as opposed to stating, "I," they will say "you."

There are a few explanations behind this. One reason is that it gives both of you a feeling of association. This is something that scholars frequently use to interface with their crowd positively. In any case, with regards to mental control, this is utilized in a progressively negative way. Psyche controllers who need to work on your self- assurance will use "you" when examining a negative story, one which can place you in an awful light. Even though you realize you didn't do this, and you are not very of the story, it goes into your psyche mind and can cause you to accept that you accomplished something comparable in your life. Subsequently, your emotions toward the individual in the story are what you are feeling toward yourself.

They Will Think for You

Individuals who need to control you intellectually will have no difficult beginning to think for you. Their stunt is regularly; they will initially begin to settle on a choice for you where it truly doesn't make a difference. You may be examining something and let them know, "I don't know what I think. Let me consider it." This is an open way for somebody who needs to control your brain. This discloses to them that you need assistance settling on a choice. Subsequently, if they step in to decide on the choice for you unobtrusively, it won't trouble you.

They will tell you something like, "I realize you are worried about everything else, so why not let me settle on the choice, and we will discuss it." Then, to appear as though they set aside an effort to settle on the choice, they will come to you somewhat later with their answer. They will act like you have a decision or act as they care about your opinion of their choice. Be that as it may, you genuinely don't have a

decision. They are merely attempting to get you to believe that they can settle on choices for you.

They will, at that point, begin settling on more choices for you, without your authorization. Be that as it may, you won't give a lot of consideration to these choices since they truly aren't excessively significant. At that point, they will quit getting some information about anything. It is when they begin to restrict your choices, notwithstanding, you, despite everything, probably won't notice because you have started to get used to them thinking for you.

Who Uses Mind Control

Mind control can be as simple as a subliminal suggestion used to steer one in the direction you want rather than the order they were going autonomously. Every day, you are exposed

to one form of mind control or another. Product placement on television and in movies. The music you hear in a store or even an elevator. Friends that are so convincing, you can't help but agree, or you find yourself always saying yes to them.

Re-education is a very optimal but controversial tool in mind control. The ability to re-educate another person's previous thought process or beliefs is possible but can take time. By repeating the same belief, idea, or thought to another person repeatedly, you impress upon them the change from their ideas towards your own. And this repetition leads to immersion in the idea or action you want them to follow.

Media Producers

Just as our five senses are our guides in life, they can also be our enemies and traitors. Our sense of sight and the visual processing areas of the brain are compelling. We almost always dream visually, even if another sense is missing, and we usually picture someone we are remembering rather than associating some other sensory input with them. This makes imagery and visual manipulation an incredibly powerful technique of media mind control.

Traditionally, media production was in the hands of companies and institutions. These manipulative entities were able to pioneer the use of visual, subliminal mind control. Examples include split-second pictures of a product or person inserted into a seemingly innocent

movie. Such split-second images, which the person perceives as nothing more than a flash of light, can take powerful control of a person's emotions. They have been used as recently as 21st-century Presidential elections.

Sound is another way in which a person is vulnerable to undetected mind control.

Both experiments and personal experience will confirm this to you. Have you ever loved a song until it stuck in your head? How easy was it to get rid of? The sound had a powerful influence over you, even though you knew it was present. The power of audio manipulation is even greater when it is undetected. Experiments have shown that if restaurant customers are exposed to music from a particular region, they are more likely to order wine from that country. When questioned, they had no idea that something as simple as the sound had steered their decision.

Lovers

People are always a product of the environment they are in. The way people are raised affects the way they act in later life. Someone raised by alcoholics has a greater chance of becoming alcoholics in adult life, or they may choose never to drink. People raised in a house where everything is prohibited may cut loose when they are finally on their own. People from different economic and religious backgrounds. People have different beliefs about what is right and wrong, what is acceptable and unacceptable. The problem comes when two people try to have a relationship, but neither wants to change their way of thinking. When that happens, there is no relationship. Just two people are living together under the same roof.

People who create and keep good, mutually satisfactory relationships with others enjoy much more success than people who do not do this. The ability to grow and maintain honest relationships is easier for some people.

Salespeople

If a salesperson asks a regular customer to write a brief endorsement of the product they buy, they will hopefully say yes. If someone asks their significant other to take some of the business cards to pass out at work, they will hopefully say yes. If you write any blog and ask another blogger to provide a link to yours on their blog, they will hopefully say yes. When enough people say yes, the business or blog will begin to grow. With even more yesses, it will continue to grow and thrive. This is the very simple basis of marketing. Marketing is nothing more than using mind control to get other people to buy something or do something beneficial. And the techniques can easily be learned.

Writers

Think of writing a guest spot for someone else who has their blog. By sending in the entire manuscript first, there is a greater risk of rejection. Begin small. Send them a paragraph or two discussing them with the idea. Then outline the idea and send that in an email. Then write the complete draft you would like them to use and send it along. When asking a customer for a testimonial, start by asking for a few lines in an email. Then ask the customer to expand those few lines into a testimonial covering at least half a typed page. The customer will soon be ready for an hour-long webcast extolling the virtues of the product and your excellent customer service skills.

Everything must have a deadline that exists. The critical word here is the word 'real.' Everyone has heard the salesperson who said to decide because the deal might not be available later or another customer was coming in, and they might get it. That is a total fabrication, and everyone knows it to be true. There is no impending other customers, and the deal is not going to disappear. There is no real sense of urgency involved. But everyone does it. There are too many situations where people are given a fake deadline by someone who thinks it will instill a great sense of urgency for completing the task. It is not only not useful but completely unneeded. It is a simple matter to create real

urgency. Only leave free things available for a finite amount of time. When asking customers for testimonials, be sure to mention the last possible day for it to be received to be used. Some people will be unable to assist but having people unable to participate is better than never beginning.

In Education

By educating impressionable children, society essentially teaches them to become "ideal" members of the community. They are taught and trained in specific ways that fulfill the government and authorities' desires and don't even think twice about it.

Advertising and Propaganda

By putting advertising and propaganda everywhere, those in control can eliminate people's feelings of self-worth and encourage them to need what is being sold instead of just wanting it. This is essentially a subliminal strategy to make people feel poorly about themselves to purchase whatever is being advertised to increase their feelings of self- worth.

Sports, Politics, Religion

The idea of these strategies is to "divide and conquer." Ultimately, each one has people placed into various categories, where they feel very strongly. As a result, they don't support one another, but instead, they are against each other. This means that they are divided, and so the authority can conquer.

How Toxic People Choose Their Favorite Victims

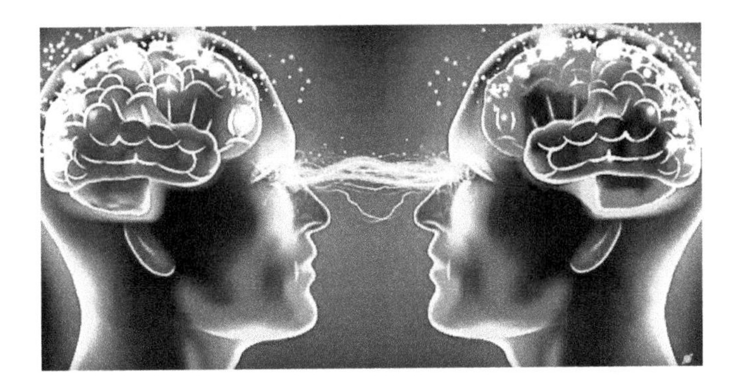

People who tend to become victims of emotional manipulation are usually weak individuals or those with low self-esteem.

It is difficult for a perfectly integrated, psychologically determined, and self-confident person to fall into the clutches of a manipulator.

The people most at risk have some weak points in which the manipulator can easily fit in.

The manipulator always studies his victims carefully, and with certain techniques, he can understand what his victim's needs are, what his desires are, and what to do to gain his trust.

In turn, victims are ready to open up to others if they are stimulated in the right way and with the right arguments.

Among the most sensitive people we have:

- very sensitive people
- people who need companionship and escape from loneliness
- fragile and insecure people
- overly empathic people
- people looking for role models
- people who take care of others
- lonely people
- people seeking approval
- people who are afraid of disappointing others
- people who always want to show a positive image of themselves

Once they fall into the trap, they cannot get out on their own and require outside help.

As time goes by, victims develop new beliefs and reject any different point of view:

- they can't imagine their life away from that of their manipulator
- their purpose is to take care of the manipulator by neglecting themselves
- confuse love and violence
- are only satisfied if they realize they have satisfied the manipulator

Purpose of mental manipulation

According to Dark Psychology, in almost all cases, a manipulator is led to perform his actions for personal purposes.

These motivations can be economical, effective, sexual, religious, and, in any case, whatever they may be, they presuppose an objective defined at the outset.

Consequently, mental manipulation is almost always carried out under the impulse of a rational and emotional drive.

Only a percentage close to zero would be cases in which the victim undergoes mental manipulation without a defined objective.

Passive and active manipulation Is mind control possible?

The reality is that the question is controversial, and there are two different points of view:

- mental manipulation is seen as a passive act
- mental manipulation is seen as an active act

The first theory supporters believe that mind control is possible, but only because there are weak or low self-esteem individuals who are prone to depend psychologically on other people.

These weak individuals, overwhelmed by thoughts, personal problems, and stress, prefer to delegate their lives to other people who can make decisions in their place.

As a result, it is easy for them to fall victim to strong personalities and charismatic leaders regardless of whether they are positive or negative leaders.

Within this group of weak individuals, some need to belong to a group of people.

In the age of social networks, it is more and more usual to find young boys and girls who ardently desire to be part of a group of people united by particular characteristics (fashionable clothes, weight loss, tests of courage, etc.).

These people tend to make decisions or adhere to currents of thought for the sole purpose of feeling part of the group.

In these cases, it is the group itself that recognizes authority, which has enormous power in plagiarizing its followers.

We can take the example of influencers who can push hundreds and hundreds of followers to purchase or take a certain attitude with a simple photograph.

Even more, fitting with mental manipulation is the Blue Whale phenomenon, a game born in Russia and spread online through chat and social networks, and that has led some guys to make the extreme gesture of suicide.

Getting out of this sort of virtual reality is very complex and impossible to carry out without a valid external help.

People who usually fall into a trap are already weak people who, with time, tend to lose their self-esteem.

The second thesis that of active manipulation is carried out by those who believe that mind control is possible regardless of whom the victim is.

According to their idea, with the right techniques and the right time available, it is possible to control any person's will, thoughts, and actions.

However, in the same way, those who can manipulate people are, in most cases, predisposed individuals with psychopathic connotations.

Consequently, we see that, in both theses, on one side or the other, there is still a problematic person.

Manipulation Psychology

Manipulation is much more morally questionable than mere persuasion, in that it is done with some degree of deception and without the best interests of those being influenced in
mind. That being said, this section will speak in terms of what a manipulator would do in a situation. At times I will frame this discourse with such statements as, "If you want to successfully manipulate someone, then you should…" It would be very easy to misinterpret this kind of framing as prescriptive, but keep in mind, in the above example, "should" is not meant to represent advocacy – it is dependent on the "if" clause of the statement. Basically, it's telling what would be advisable if your goal was to manipulate, not suggesting that you ever should.

How Psychology Correlate with Manipulation

Three psychological conditions that are associated with manipulation are narcissism, psychosis, and sociopathy. Before talking about how the different ways manipulators might attempt to influence others, we'll give some background on these underlying psychological conditions. A narcissist suffers from the narcissistic personality disorder, or NPD. As is true of many psychological measures, NPD can be seen as existing on a spectrum; people might have it to differing degrees.

The overarching characteristics of NPD include the following:

- A grandiose self-image that might exaggerate the sufferer's importance, talent, or achievements.
- A lack of empathy for other people.
- A strong need for admiration from others.
- Unrealistic fantasies of power, achievement, success, or idealized love.
- A belief in a unique or special status that can only be understood by an elite few.

- An expectation of special or deferential treatment.
- A general attitude of arrogance.
- An envy of others or delusional belief that he or she is subject to the envy of others.
- A willingness to exploit or manipulate others.

Obviously, this last characteristic is the most relevant to our purposes, but most of the others point towards the basic psychology of narcissism that so enables manipulation. The strong egocentric framing, the delusions of grandeur and the lack of empathy lead to a personality perfectly willing to pursue self-interested behavior at the expense of others.

Within the broader category of narcissists there is a spectrum of subtypes that ranges from exhibitionist narcissists to closeted ones. There are some who are unapologetically abusive and vindictive and others that are thoughtful and capable of remorse. The more fully a narcissist conforms to the above list of characteristics, the more likely they are to be considered a malignant narcissist; one capable of inflicting harm.

Antisocial Personality Disorder, or APD, is the clinical diagnosis for sociopathy. Like narcissism, sociopathy tends to be a long-lived condition, often permanent, and has extensive effects. To meet the clinical definition, an APD sufferer must demonstrate a conduct disorder by the age of fifteen which includes at least four of the following characteristics.

- Inability to maintain consistency in work or schoolwork.
- Ignored social norms. May engage in illegal behavior.
- A casual disregard for safety concerns, either concerning the self or others.
- Irresponsibility, as seen on the job or in a failure to honor obligations of a financial nature.
- Difficulty in maintaining monogamous relationships for over a year.
- Impulsive and lacking in ambition or planning, tending to proceed without clear goals.
- Easily irritated and aggressive or violent.
- A lack of concern with honesty. This might be demonstrated by continuous lying, conning people, reneging on debts, or using aliases.

- Lacks remorse and feels justified in having hurt, mistreated, or stolen
- from another

These first two categories are similar in both their positive and negative characteristics. Either can be intelligent, charismatic or successful. At the same time, narcissists and sociopaths can both be controlling, irresponsible, and proceed with an exaggerated sense of entitlement. Both can be abusive and both tend to refuse to take responsibility for this behavior. They tend to produce justifications for their worst behaviors. On a core level, both tend to lack empathy, although they may be able to fake empathetic reactions when it benefits them.

Although they do have similarities, there are important distinctions between the two categories. In the Venn diagram of disorders, all sociopaths are narcissists, but not all narcissists qualify as sociopaths. They differ in motivations. Sociopaths tend to be more cunningly manipulative, because everything isn't personal for them. Narcissists are ego-driven, but for sociopaths, the ego isn't a factor. They can, in

fact, be viewed as lacking a real personality. They can inhabit any persona that is convenient for a given situation. This makes sociopaths harder to identify. Their tactics shift relative to a situation. They may try to win the approval of others, but only if it acts in service of their goals. They can perform humility, seeming to show remorse, but again, this is strategic and based on an agenda. Sociopaths act with a higher level of planning and calculation. Even aggression might be premeditated.

Narcissists are more reactive. They may employ lies and attempt to intimidate, but are more likely to do it without a game plan, simply reacting to a situation driven by their overactive egos. A narcissist will work towards their own success or goal of achieving some measure of perfection. They are perfectly willing to exploit others as they pursue these goals, but the manipulation is secondary and directed towards personal interests and a self-centered worldview.

Both personality types are motivated by their own interests, but only narcissists truly care what others think of them. The admiration of others is gratifying. This introduces a codependent aspect to their personalities, making them capable of being manipulated themselves.

The third category of manipulative personality type worth discussing includes psychopaths. Psychosis is distinguished by a difficulty in distinguishing fantasy and reality. Sufferers may be delusional or hallucinatory. The following list contains the common traits of psychopaths. While many of these are shared in our previous two categories, remember the important distinguishing factors defining psychosis.

- Exaggerated sense of self-worth
- Fleeting or shallow emotions
- Inability to form realistic long-term goals
- Impulsive behavior
- Inability to control behavior
- Superficially charming and glib
- Being conning and manipulative

Psychopaths tend to mislead and manipulate others through dishonestly and a superficial charm that can come off as glib. Psychopaths may mislead in order to gain an advantage or they might be motivated to deceive and abuse merely for their own amusement. Some simply cannot resist these negative impulses. Typically, psychopaths have developed these characteristics over the course of their entire lives. They have incorporated them into an often basically functional routine. Sometimes the traits are even externally reinforced to an extent. As a result, they don't see these characteristics as problematic. In fact, people with high levels of psychopathy often are largely unconcerned with how they are perceived, exhibiting a willingness to demonstrate their fearlessness even if it means they will be overtly perceived as dominating.

They also tend not to worry about the consequences of their actions on others. As they tend to have very little empathy, impacts such as these seem irrelevant. They do, in fact, feel that their motivations are of innately greater concerns than those of others. This contributes to delusional regard of their own motives and actions, as if they served some higher purpose.

The delusional nature of psychosis also contributes to the fact that psychotics often believe their own lies. Lying is natural to highly psychotic people, but that does not mean they are always conscious that they are lying. Their detachment from reality can lead them to feel and believe what they are saying even when it is motivated by conscious deception. All of these characteristics naturally contribute to a high correlation of manipulative behavior and diagnoses of psychosis.

We'll refer back to all of these conditions on occasion, but it is worth noting that one does not need to be diagnosed with one of them in order to be a manipulator. People with other psychological conditions or those who are in perfect mental health are perfectly capable of engaging in manipulative behavior under the right circumstances.

The Body beyond Words

Your body language is a significant factor in how you approach others. Listening skills are a must and essential for developing good relationships with clients in many careers, particularly
those you support others.

Whether you help people improve their ties, provide people with feedback for business success, or advise on some other issue, they see your body language and show strong listening skills. It makes people more relaxed.

Poor body language could cause you to lose something extraordinary. Your body language can make others feel important as you give them the attention they need.

It is essential to know the bad listener's symptoms and try to get rid of them. You don't want to hear what he or she is doing. This most definitely would lead to the end of the relationship, which may lead to major business losses.

So, what can you do to start sending positive signals to the person with whom you speak?

At the time of contact, we come to the body position. You need to take an open position. You must never hold your arms or legs close, or the other person will think you don't want to hear his point.

If you lean forward when talking to others, the body language suggests that you pay more attention to what he is doing. In comparison, leaning away means you don't have much interest at all.

Communication with the eye is the most significant aspect. Try to keep the eye in contact at all times. If you continue to look away, it shows that you have little interest in the matter and feel awkward. Don't try to be too rigid.

You shouldn't be too formal to speak to anyone, either. If you believe your body has experienced significant losses in the past, you should start following the tips above immediately.

Body Language Talks all the time:

The moment you leave your house, your body language starts to speak for you. Even you don't talk, while you're standing, sitting, and using your hands, that's what some see as a contact.

If you have no good knowledge of body language, your language will often not correspond to your purposes, and people will get the wrong message. If your body language is inconsistent with what your motives are, you will lose your reputation.

How to maintain credibility

We should learn a bit more about body language, be more trustworthy and professional in others' eyes. Make your entry as good as possible when you reach your customer for any form of company.

How can you do that?

You can start by talking about the company once you reach the customer's premises. Taking papers or checking the case gives a negative message.

Another important lesson in body language is to shake hands warmly and firmly. We come next to the selection of the chair to sit on. You should never say that you would sit when the other person asks you.

Instead, pick the most suitable chair and sit right away. Never make the mistake of sitting too near or too far from the customer. How shy person needs to sit a little more than an outgoing person. The optimal size, however, is between 20 and 50 inches. You can lean towards the consumer if you try to emphasize a specific argument.

Importance of Eye and Voice Contact:

Another important body language is eye contact. Communication with your eyes and a smile on your face will show you as true, sincere, and transparent. Slight eye contact and a glance here and there will always give you the message that you don't have enough confidence. But also stop continually looking at the other person, as this makes the consumer feel very awkward. Try to talk in your normal voice still. If your voice is enthusiastic, it will quickly take the customer's attention.

Body language: what are the different postures?

You should consider your body language to be outstanding when you speak in your usual tone and when the volume is also regular.A well- modulated voice with a regular rhythm and pace shows interest and passion. The words you use during your speech should be as simple as possible. When you use 'um' or 'a' or clear your throat excessively, it tells a message that you are nervous.

Emphasis on Posture and Manipulation

You should also concentrate on your movements and postures if you want to improve your body language. Here are some easy suggestions for enhancing posture. You should always walk freely, take fast, fixed steps with swinging arms, but you should stand upright. If you hold the other person's eye in contact, cup your chin between your finger and thumb, cross the nose bridge with your hands, or reach the chin, you show that you are thinking about what is said.

Some negative indicators of body language

Bad body language involves anxious gestures that suggest carelessness. You have to stop looking nervous and keep yourself aware of your body language message.

For example, when you fold your arms, cross the legs, try to catch lint that is not on your skin, or shift your hands on the face, you express your disagreement with others. Blinking your eyes repeatedly, coughing multiple times, looking at the conversation's time, and seeing various locations by rapidly moving your eyes indicate negative behavior.

Frustration

You demonstrate your anger with your body language when you point at something with your index finger. Similarly, wringing your mouth, playing with the hair, and tightly clamping your mouth are signs of anger. Now, how can someone prove that he's bored?

If the listener's eyes aren't fixed on the person who talks, whether he is distracted or interested in doing anything more than listen to what is said, he shows that he's getting bored. The value of body language increases even more when you encounter people from different cultures.

The Importance of Body Language

Language is the most critical part of what we communicate. It is usually more reliable than the words we use.

Some of the things we say about our bodies will help us to improve why we say it. When simply saying, "I don't know," the following movements have little to add. We should turn our hands face up in front of us by lifting our brows and turning our eyes while slightly gripping our bottom lip and looking sideways. Now we have made someone laugh and maybe lifted a little of the burden off ourselves or the other guy, who was a bit worried that we didn't know something we didn't know.

Furthermore, paying attention to someone's body language will help us determine when someone does not tell us the truth. Here are some signs that someone might lie. Sometimes, a person who does not know

the truth would not want to contact the eye because the eyes are windows to his lying souls.

There are, however, other signs of deceit. A person who does not speak the full truth will clear his throat, stump or change his or her voice as though trying to distract attention from his or her lie or to pause so that they can think of a valid response or plausible explanation.

Moreover, taps or bounces, blush, place your hand on your forehead, turn away, or raise your shoulders may mean that you don't have a conversation and don't know the truth.

Another essential feature of corporal language is to communicate our thoughts on what we speak on. The body language will help us decide how someone thinks about what they say.

For example, an individual might tell her boss that she is happy to take the matter into account, but her body language may show that she is not happy about it. This can be an essential move that can help a manager decide who the right person to do this role is.

In a work interview, body language may be the deciding factor. If the applicant's corporate language indicates he is comfortable with the subject matter and has faith, he is more likely to get the job, particularly in this difficult job market. We spoke earlier that some body language is considered tense and out of reach. These are some of the same features that make a job seeker less confident and relaxed.

In a relationship, one's body language may show that one pays attention or doesn't care what the other person says. Moving towards the demonstrates that the person needs to hear what the other person says. Leaning back will prove he was unselfish or thought superior.

Reaching forward and standing near during conversation can mean that someone is actively trying to convince or control the conversation. When you hear someone without eye contact, you don't

pay attention but wait for your chance to speak. This gives your friend the impression that it doesn't matter what they say, and they won't listen closely to you when it's up to you to speak.

Let's Analyze Specifically The Code Of NLP

What is NLP?

NLP stands for 'Neuro-Linguistic Programming,' and is the study of excellence. It glares deep into what it means for people to be great and for people to achieve high levels of
success. It looks to figure out exactly what it is that those who succeed do by creating a model of their behaviors, of their unconscious patterns, and how they approach certain problems. On top of that, it is the study of how language and thoughts can be used to transform the mind. It uses everything from hypnosis, to visualization, to therapeutic measures. It is the user manual of the human brain.

John Grinder and Richard Bandler discovered it as the first new form of psychotherapy and created it in the 1970s as they studied Milton Erickson and Virginia Satir, two of the most successful therapists of the time. The transformations these two people achieved with their

patients became things of legend. Milton Erickson used hypnosis to help patients make a rapid transformation. His use of hypnosis transformed psychotherapy and legitimized hypnosis as a real, useful, and powerful tool recognized by the American Medical Association.

Virginia Satir is considered the mother of family therapy, discovering a quick way to helping people work through their craziness, by oftentimes working with them in a family environment. She once said, "People hardly ever seemed as crazy when you saw them together with their family." Using a process of meta-analysis, she would often deconstruct what people are saying and thinking. Much of these early methods have made their way into a host of other therapeutic methods.

NLP oftentimes is ignored by the mainstream for its broad applications, but it is its broad applications that often help so many people and makes NLP one of the most powerful tools anyone can learn in their life. People have used the techniques to transform their lives and take greater control of themselves as well as using a host of other techniques to better motivate and persuade people.

We will go through some of the hallmark methodologies that will lay out some basic actions you can take to start taking advantage of these abilities.

The techniques that we will be laid out for you, from conversational hypnosis to reframing, to the famous and powerful swish pattern, are powerful tools that will hopefully give you the control and power you deserve in your life.

How NLP Works

If you are just coming across this topic for the first time, NLP may appear or seem like magic or hypnosis. When a person is undergoing

therapy, this topic digs deep into the unconscious mind of the patient and filters through different layers of beliefs and the person's approach or perception of life to deduce the early childhood experiences that are responsible for a behavioral pattern.

In NLP, it is believed that everyone has the resources that are needed for positive changes in their own lives. The technique adopted here is meant to help in facilitating these changes.

Usually, when NLP is taught, it is done in a pyramidal structure. However, the most advanced techniques are left for those multi- thousand-dollar seminars. An attempt to explain this complicated subject is to state that the NLPer (as those who use NLP will often call themselves) is always paying keen attention to the person they are working on/with.

Usually, there is a large majority of NLPers that are therapists, and they are very likely to be well-meaning people. They achieve their aims by paying attention to those subtle cues like the movement of the eyes, flushing of the skin, dilation of the pupil, and subtle nervous tics. It is easy for an NLP user to quickly determine the following:

- The side of the brain that the person uses predominantly.
- The sense (smell, sight, etc.) that is more dominant in a person's brain.
- The way the person's brain stores and makes use of information (the

NLPer can deduce all this from the person's eye movement).

- When they are telling a lie or concocting information.

When the NLP user has successfully gathered all this information, they begin to mimic the client slowly and subtly by not only taking on their body language but also by imitating their speech and mannerisms, so

that they begin to talk with the language patterns that are aimed at targeting the primary senses of the client. They will typically fake the social cues that will easily make someone let their guard down so that they become very open and suggestible.

For example, when a person's sense of sight is their most dominant sense, the NLPer will use a language that is very laden with visual metaphors to speak with them. They will say things like: "Do you see what I am talking about?" or "Why not look at it this way?" For a person that has a more dominant sense of hearing, he will be approached with an auditory language like: "Listen to me" or "I can hear where you're coming from."

To create a rapport, the NLPer mirror the body language and the linguistic patterns of the other person. This rapport is a mental and physiological state which a human being gets into when they lose guard of their social senses. It is done when they begin to feel like the other person who they are conversing with is just like them.

Once the NLPer has achieved this rapport, they will take charge of the interaction by leading it mildly and subtly. Thanks to the fact that they have already mirrored the other person, they will now begin to make some subtle changes to gain a certain influence on the behavior of the person. This is also combined with some similar subtle language patterns which lead to questions and a whole phase of some other techniques.

At this point, the NLPer will be able to tweak and twist the person to whichever direction they desire. This only happens if the other person can't deduce that something is going on because they assume everything that is occurring is happening organically, or that they have given consent to everything.

What this means is that it is quite hard to make use of NLP to get other people to act out of character, but it can be used to get a person to give responses within their normal range of character. This may come in the form of getting them to donate to a charitable cause, finally making the decision they had been putting off, or getting them to go home with you for the night, if they had considered it at some previous point.

At this point, what the NLP user seeks to do may be to either elicit or anchor. When they are eliciting, they make use of both leading and language to get the person to an emotional state of say, sadness. Once they can elicit this state, they can then lead it on with a physical cue by touching the other person's shoulder for example.

According to theory, whenever the NLP user touches the person's shoulder in the same manner, the same emotional state will resurface if they do it again. However, this is only made possible by the successful conditioning of the other person.

When undergoing NLP therapy, the therapist can adopt a content-free approach, which means the therapist can work effectively without taking a critical look at the problem or without even knowing about the problem at all. This means that there is room for privacy for the client as the therapist does not need to be told about whichever event took place, or whatever issue happened in the past.

Also, before the commencement of the therapy, there is an agreement that ensures that the therapist cannot disclose any information, hence the interaction between the therapist and the client remains confidential.

In NLP, there is the belief in the need for the perfection of the nature of human creation, so every client is encouraged to recognize the sensitivity of the senses and make use of them in responding to specific problems. NLP also holds the belief that the mind can find cures to diseases and sicknesses.

The techniques employed by NLP have to do with a noninvasive, medicine-free therapy that enables the client to find out new ways of handling emotional issues such as low self-esteem, lack of confidence, anxiety, and destructive relationship patterns. It is also a successful tool in effective bereavement counseling.

With its roots in the field of behavioral science, which was developed by Skinner, Pavlov, and Thorndike, NLP makes use of the combination of physiology and the unconscious mind to bring about change in the thought process and ultimately in the behavior of a person.

The Importance Of NLP

Neuro-Linguistic Programming is not only necessary for the understanding of a person's being, but it also helps in the understanding of the way an individual is. It helps a person to get deep into the root cause of the problem, as well as the foundation of their being.

Here are some other reasons why NLP is important:

- It helps people take responsibility for the things that they feel they may not be able to control. With the help of NLP, a person can change the way they react to events of the past and have a certain level of control over their future.

- People need to be aware of the body language of the members of their inner circle, as well as those who they seek to do business with. With NLP, it is possible to make use of the language with both control and purpose, and with this, it is possible to have control over your life.

Remember, you cannot expect to make the same mistakes using the same mindset and hope to get different results. During an NLP session, the focus is placed entirely on the client as they are made the subject. This helps a lot because, at the point where a person can deal with his or herself as a person, they gain more clarity into his or her dealings with other people.

- It helps to improve finances, sales performance, marriage, health issues, parenting, customer service, and every other aspect and phase of life. This is because it helps in the holistic improvement of an individual and when a person is whole, his interactions and relationship with himself and other people become whole as well.

- It assists in targeting your beliefs, thoughts, and values and helps with the targeting of a person's brain functions, as well as developing certain behaviors. It also shapes the way these behaviors metamorphoses into habits, and how the habits change to actions which in turn comes as results.

NLP applies to different vocations and professions. This is a tool that is very important in the mastery of sales, personal development experts and self-help, teaching, communication, parenting, and other facets of life.

Conscious And Subconscious

Modify The Subconscious Via NLP

Here we have some of the best techniques by which you could change your subconscious via NLP.

Association – Music

For many people, music is an essential part of their life. The genre doesn't matter, as long as you enjoy it. Music has sway over us that not many things do. It influences the way we feel, which is why music therapy is effective. Music helps with our feelings, which is why it is a technique of association in NLP.

This exercise links a song with self-confidence. You probably have a song that makes you feel on top of the world. Take a minute and go through your playlist to find a song that makes you feel confident or inspired. Once you choose a song, hum, or sing it whenever you feel down, if you want, you can pretend to play an imaginary guitar to feel better.

The Trigger

This is a visualization exercise. Sit in a quiet spot and close your eyes. Make sure that your breathing is regular and clear your mind. When you feel calm, open your eyes and visualize a mirror image of yourself in front of you. This person is self-assured, successful, and reacts rationally and clearly to stressful situations and problems. Focus on your clone and study how they behave.

After you have thoroughly analyzed them, put yourself in their shoes. Feel their strength and confidence coursing through your body. This is your trigger from now on. Whenever you want to feel powerful, repeat this exercise. The more you practice, the stronger this feeling will become.

Daily Affirmations

Start your day positively with daily affirmations. It is essential to take time in the morning to think about what you like about yourself. Remember that you are the only one that has the power to do what you want. If you want to achieve something, then instead of telling yourself that you will get there someday, you need to feel like you are already there. Think about yourself as the person you want to be.

Kill the Voices

We all experience moments of weakness, where a nagging voice in our heads tells us we aren't good enough. It reminds us we're unlikable or haven't achieved anything worthwhile yet. This voice spouts destructive thoughts that suck away our motivation.

Think of the last time you heard this voice. Do you recognize it? Is it yours or someone else's? When you have a clear idea of whose voice it is, it is time to change the script.

Think of how the voice would sound if it belonged to Donald Duck or any other Disney character. Imagine a funny scene where the voice speaker tries to sound profound but cannot pull it off. This will render the nagging voice ineffective. It is like how the wizards in Harry Potter defeat a Boggart. The Boggart can materialize their worst fear, but when they imagine it in a funny context, the Boggart loses all its power.

The Whiteout

We all have memories that surface at inappropriate times, making us feel uncomfortable and preventing us from giving our best. They are deeply rooted in our subconscious because we associate strong negative feelings with them. The whiteout technique will help you stop thinking about these memories.

First, think of a memory that makes you feel uncomfortable. It can be something embarrassing or humiliating or heartbreaking. Once you have a clear image established in your mind, turn up the brightness of the image quickly, so that the image goes white.

After this, pause for a second and think of something entirely different. Repeat the process quickly at least six or seven times, then pause to see what happens. When you think of the uncomfortable memory again, it will either whiteout by itself, or you won't be able to see it clearly at all. Adding a sound effect to the whiteout process can help.

Make sure to pause between each cycle so that your brain doesn't create a loop of the image and the whiteout.

Grounding

This technique develops your confidence and a solid foundation on which to build. You must be barefoot for this technique, but if this is not possible, make sure you are not wearing high heels.

Stand up straight, keeping your feet shoulder-width apart and flat on the ground. Then move your hips slightly forward and feel your stomach and thigh muscles tense, your arms loose at your sides. Now unlock—but don't bend—your knees, and take a few deep, long breaths, focusing your eyes in front of you. Notice how you feel.

Practice this posture a few times a day, and once you are comfortable, try moving around in it. Make sure you are breathing as you move. It will feel natural after you've familiarized yourself with it and will help you stay mentally and physically grounded in reality.

Take Words at Face Value

One of the secrets to mastering NLP is to take what people say literally, which might seem absurd. After all, we don't always mean what we say. Some things are said just for dramatic value, while others are intended to stress something.

But if you really want to understand the psychology of someone you are talking to, you must take them literally. People will tell you what you need to know in the first couple of minutes. You must exhibit openness and ask the right questions. If someone tells you they can't envision themselves losing weight, you must not try to convince them that they can. Instead, you can try to make them see things from a different perspective.

See, people don't like to "lose" things. If that is what you set as a goal, you are setting yourself up for failure in most cases. People also don't process negatives as well as process positives. So, telling someone not to think about an elephant will result in just the opposite. It is wired into our neurology.

Experimentation

Our subconscious dictates how we communicate with others. When we talk, we subconsciously have a goal in mind, whether we are aware of it or not, and our communication is aimed at fulfilling that goal.

Remember your last conversation on the phone. You were probably not paying attention to the conversation at least half the time. Your mind was busy forming coherent thoughts that manifested into proper

replies. This is because language, vocabulary, and grammar are deeply embedded in your subconscious.

To become skilled at communication, you must experiment with this. Think of yourself as a baby who does not yet have a concept of failure. Try different phrases and words as you interact with someone you trust, maybe a fellow NLP-practicing buddy. Notice how you get better with time.

Anchoring

Anchoring is a useful NLP technique for inducing a particular mental state or emotion. It helps you enter a mental frame of happiness, relaxation, focus, or another state you desire. It usually requires a touch, gesture, or verbal cue: an "anchor." This anchor acts as a bookmark for you to recall an emotion or state of mind at will.

To understand how anchoring works, let's look at an example. For this, think about a time when you felt happy. It can be when you won a race, or when you had a baby, or maybe when you had your first kiss. Once you have a memory in mind, could you think of the moments leading up to it? What happened before the happy moment? Create a story, and picture it in your head, recalling your feelings at the time. Be as vivid and detailed as possible.

When you are at the pinnacle of such feelings, take your index and middle fingers on your left hand and place them in your right hand. Then give two quick, gentle squeezes to the fingers. When you squeeze them for the second time, picture the happy moment in a larger frame, as if it were closer to you than before. Imagine the feeling of growing exponentially and getting stronger inside you.

After this, it is only a game of repetition. Describe the feeling again, recalling exactly what you felt at that moment. Then squeeze the same two fingers with your right hand and expand the picture on the second squeeze. Repeat this process at least five times. You will notice that the happy feeling doubles by itself without you forcing it after enough repetition.

Now you have laid the anchor. When you become adept at this technique, you can easily recall this anchor at any time by squeezing your fingers twice. You will feel happy instantly just by recalling your anchor.

Pacing

You can use pacing to influence others. With this technique, you can enter another person's model of reality on their terms. It is like walking next to someone at their pace. Once you pace them, establish a rapport with them, and understand them, you next need to lead them using your rapport to influence them.

For example, if you need to persuade someone to act in a particular way, you first need to understand why they act the way they do. Once you understand this, you can then work on establishing a rapport with them. Find common ground and use it to understand them. Once the other person realizes that you think alike, they will become more receptive to your suggestions.

The Pizza-Walk

From a young age, we are taught to think of mistakes as dangerous. It is part of our social conditioning. And for this reason, our nervous system protects us from dangerous situations. We must understand, though, that we learn from making mistakes. If you want to be skilled at NLP, you must give yourself the chance to fail.

Many people are hesitant when they want to try something new. To remove hesitation, I like to suggest a method called the Pizza-Walk Experience. It costs almost nothing and can be done anywhere. This

exercise will help you leave all the unnecessary hesitation that holds you back from doing your best.

Think about the areas in your life in which you hesitate. After this, go to any commercial space of your choosing, like a restaurant or gas station, and ask for something completely absurd that you are sure you won't find there. Keep a straight face when you request it and be polite and non-threatening. Repeat this process at least twice in the following week. Notice the change in your hesitation.

It is that simple. Hesitation is one of the most significant barriers to learning, and with this technique, you can remove it from your life. Are you afraid to ask out a girl you like? Want to apply for a new job in a local tech company but are not sure if you are good enough? Go for the pizza-walk then see the change.

Mirroring

As the name suggests, you need to copy another person's gestures, tone of voice, mannerisms, or catchphrases in mirroring.

CONCLUSION

Thank you for reading all this book!

Thank you for making it to the end. Manipulation commonly occurs when an individual is used for the benefit of others. It is a situation where the manipulator comes up with an
imbalance of power and goes ahead to exploit his victim to serve their main agendas. Those who are manipulative are the kind of people who will disguise their desires and interests as yours. They will undertake all they can to make you believe that their own opinions are the objective facts. They act as if they are cornered. Manipulators will pretend to offer assistance to improve your attitude, performance and promise that they will help you improve your life in general. That is all that they want you to believe. The hidden truth is that these people's main aim is to control you and not control you, as they want you to feel. They don't want to make your life better,

but to change you. They also want to validate their lives and make sure that you don't outgrow them.

Once you have given these characters back to your life, getting rid of them will not be easy. They will appear to flip flop on issues and act so slippery when you want to hold them accountable. They also tend to promise you help that doesn't seem to be near.

You have already taken a step towards your improvement.

Best wishes!

CPSIA information can be obtained
at www.ICGtesting.com
Printed in the USA
LVHW052352070421
683722LV00002B/496